Home Places

VOLUME 31

SUN TRACKS

. . . .

An American Indian Literary Series

Series Editor

Ofelia Zepeda

Editorial Committee

Vine Deloria, Jr.

Larry Evers

Joy Harjo

N. Scott Momaday

Emory Sekaquaptewa

Leslie Marmon Silko

HOME PLACES

Contemporary Native American Writing from Sun Tracks

EDITED BY

LARRY EVERS AND OFELIA ZEPEDA

THE UNIVERSITY OF ARIZONA PRESS

Tucson & London

Publication of this book is made possible in part by a grant from the Arizona Commission on the Arts through appropriations from the Arizona State Legislature and grants from the National Endowment for the Arts.

The University of Arizona Press
Copyright © 1995
The Arizona Board of Regents
All rights reserved

99 98 97 96 95   5 4 3 2 1

Library of Congress Cataloging-in-Publication Data

Home places : contemporary Native American writing from sun tracks /
edited by Larry Evers and Ofelia Zepeda.
p.   cm. – (Sun tracks ; v. 31)
ISBN 0-8165-1521-2 (alk. paper). –
ISBN 0-8165-1522-0 (pbk. : alk. paper)
1. Indians of North America—United States—Literary collections.
2. American literature—Indian authors.   3. American
literature—20th century.   I. Evers, Larry.   II. Zepeda, Ofelia.
III. Series.
PS501.S85   vol. 31
[PS508.I5]   94-18729
810.8'0897'09045—dc20   CIP

British Cataloguing-in-Publication Data
A catalogue record for this book is available from the British Library.

Contents

Home Places: An Introduction

What has nourished Native peoples on this continent since time im-
memorial are wellsprings of creativity. Inseparable from the land, these
sources feed an idea of the continent that predates the earliest European
presence. Cycles of conquest have tested indigenous communities for
more than five hundred years. Still, a nourishing fountainhead remains.
"Down at the source," Havasupai singer Dan Hanna assures us, "a spring
will always be there."

This idea of the continent is not difficult to name. For native peoples
this is home, an earth house, a place to live within ever-widening webs
of community that spin out to include not just humans but all the living
things of the natural world. As we write, at least three hundred Native
American groups—variously called tribes, nations, bands, or peoples—
continue to inhabit home places in North America. As Edward H. Spicer
notes in *The American Indians* (1982), "nearly as many Indian tribes
exist in the 20th century as when Europeans first encountered them in
the 1600s." That North America continues to be such a home place for
Native American peoples is a fact that is, for many, too convenient to
forget. Joy Harjo cautions: "My house is the red earth; it could be the
center of the world. I've heard New York, Paris, or Tokyo called the center of the world, but I say it is magnificently humble. You could drive by
and miss it."

Home Places gathers stories, songs, and poems about Native American home places from nineteen Native American singers, tellers, and
writers. To say that these verbal artists are Native American is not to

say that they are monocultural or monolingual. The homes they write about sustain such varied tribal communities as the Creek, the Osage, the Tohono O'odham, the Diné, and the Yoemem. Moreover, to recognize these storytellers, singers, and writers as tribal is not to say that they are necessarily rural or unsophisticated. Such equations fall apart in this work, and with them the careless divisions of Native America into reservation and urban communities. Indeed, most of the writers published here have traveled widely and have lived in major metropolitan centers.

The work we have selected for *Home Places* spans a range of genres that in recent years have come to be called collectively "American Indian Literature": speeches, songs, stories from oral tradition, autobiographical writing, poetry, and fiction. The range of work that we have included is deliberate. We want this collection to suggest the continuum of imaginative verbal expression that is produced and enjoyed in Native American communities at the end of the twentieth century. It is important in this regard to notice that the work is "contemporary" in this sense: it has almost all been performed or written in the last twenty years. The common division of Native American literary expression into traditional literature and contemporary literature is frequently misleading in that it suggests a vanishing oral tradition that is giving way to writing. The songs and stories that we have included from George Blueeyes, Dan Hanna, Felipe S. Molina, Daniel Lopez, and others are eloquent demonstrations of the continuing presence of the oral tradition in contemporary Native American communities.

That some of the contemporary stories and songs appear here bilingually, in both a Native American language and English, may startle and challenge some readers. Yet the five Native languages represented in this collection—Diné, Tohono O'odham, Yoemem, Havasupai, and Maricopa—are but a few of the indigenous languages that continue to be used in Native America. A recent survey conducted by Michael Krauss ("The World's Languages in Crisis," *Language* 68 [1992]: 4–10) indicates that at least 180 indigenous languages continue to be spoken in the United States. Despite the pervasiveness of English, many Native American verbal artists continue to work in their Native languages. Indeed, it seems that during the 1980s and 1990s more and more writers from Native American communities have chosen to work in their native languages.

All the work we have gathered in this collection was published in Sun Tracks, a project that began as an American Indian literary magazine and that has evolved over the years into a series of books sponsored by the American Indian Studies Program and the Department of English at the University of Arizona and published by the University of Arizona Press. We concluded that a collection of work from the series would be a good way to celebrate twenty-five years of publishing Sun Tracks. Through its many transformations, Sun Tracks has consistently attempted to create opportunities for both established and emerging Native American writers to publish their work in the languages and forms of their choice. The diversity of languages and genres represented in this collection suggests how wide-ranging those choices may be. An essay at the end of this book gives a brief history of Sun Tracks and a checklist of what has been published thus far. We make no attempt to be comprehensive with this collection. This is not an effort to present the "best of" or the "most representative" work from Sun Tracks. Such an anthology would be so large and, in this time of ever-rising paper and printing costs, so expensive as to prevent it reaching a wide audience. Instead, our intention here is to celebrate our continuing publishing project by making something new out of some work we have enjoyed publishing along the way. From the rich plurality of culture and language available to us, then, we selected work for this collection with a desire to celebrate a central theme in contemporary Native American writing: home places.

Home places are figured in many ways in the work we have gathered here. Some of the singers, storytellers, and writers define the home place as a center of established values, marked, as in the Navajo story of George Blueeyes, by a rim of sacred mountains; or, as in the Havasu-

pai song of Dan Hanna, by significant boulders "down at the source";
or again, as in the deer song of Felipe S. Molina, by the more inclusive
cultural geography of the *huya ania*, the wilderness world of the Yoemem people, home place to *saila maso*, the deer they know as their Little
Brother. The physical geography etched in the traditional words of these
stories and songs defines the home places. Only from the vantage of
a Tohono O'odham home place could Daniel Lopez sing of the Lonely
Mountain on the horizon. Only at Coso Hot Springs, Simon J. Ortiz
tells us, can Shoshone people experience the healing power of their home
place. Other stories and songs evoke more elusive, sometimes unsettled,
but ever beckoning formulations of a native home place. What beckons
is the promise of home places reclaimed but not yet fully realized. Lance
Henson's "Glimpses of Home" is an example. In Joy Harjo's "My house
is the red earth," *home* is defined as a place to defend against those who
would reduce it to insignificance. Elizabeth Woody's "In Memory of
Crossing the Columbia" remembers a home that must be pulled from
deep beneath the waters of the Columbia River. Wendy Rose remembers
her search for "the endangered roots of a person" as a sleepless night
in a Phoenix hotel. Georgiana Valoyce-Sanchez searches with uncom-
promising queries of her parents. Ramona Wilson works to recognize
how migrations fit in with her home place. Linda Hogan finds subtle
connections that promise home by following water lines. Still other
writers present stories of belonging, stories that celebrate the restorative
potential of Native home places. Luci Tapahonso's "The Motion of Songs
Rising" and Carter Revard's "An Eagle Nation" exemplify this idea.

It must be said that the meanings of the works we have included are
by no means limited to variations on the theme of home places that we
have sketched. We are confident that all the writers gathered here ask
is that you pay attention, that you listen. "That's the place Indians talk
about," writes Simon J. Ortiz,

Listen,

that's the way you hear.
Pretty soon, you can hear it,
coming far away
deep in the ground, deep down there coming,
the voice of the power coming, closer and closer.
Listen, that's the way you hear it.
From the earth,
the moving power of the voice
and the People talking.
Praying, you know, singing soft too.

Hearing,

that's the way you listen.

Home Places asks you to listen to Native American singers, storytellers, and writers, and in this way to celebrate the wellsprings of creativity that continue to flow from the home places in Native America.

Larry Evers and Ofelia Zepeda

Home Places

SIMON J. ORTIZ

. . . .

That's the Place Indians Talk About

At a meeting in California I was talking with an elder Paiute man. He
had been a rangerider and a migrant laborer. He spoke about Coso Hot
Springs, a sacred and healing place for the Shoshonean peoples, enclosed
within the China Lake Naval Station. Like Los Alamos Scientific Labora-
tories in New Mexico, the naval station is a center for the development,
experimentation, and testing of U.S. military weapons. The elder man,
wearing thick glasses and a cowboy hat, said, "That's the place Indians
talk about."

We go up there and camp.
Several days, we stay there.
We have to take horses, wagons,
or walk.
And we would stay
for the days we have to.

The Coso Hot Springs would talk to us.
And we would talk to it.
The People have to talk to it.
That's the place Indians talk about. That's the place.

Children, women, men,
we would all go up there.
You drink that water, it makes you well.

1

You put it on your hands, face, all over,
and you get well, all well.
That's the place Indians talk about,
the Coso Hot Springs the People go to.

You take a flint like this,
a hard stone in your hand,
and you give it like this.
When you pray.
When you sing.
When you talk to the hot springs.
You talk with it when it talks to you.

Something from there,
from down in there is talking to you.
You could hear it.
You listen.

       Listen.
You can hear it.
The stones in the earth rattling together.

The stones down there moving around each other.
When we pray.
When we sing.
When we talk with the stones
rattling in the ground
and the stones moving in the ground.
That's the place Indians talk about.

Oh,
we stay there for some days.
You could hear it talking.
From far,

from far away inside, the moving power.
From far away, coming to us,
coming to us pretty soon.
Getting closer, getting close,
the power is getting close,
and the ground is hot and shaking.

Something is doing that
and the People know that.
They have to keep talking.
Praying, that's the Indian way.
Singing, that's the Indian way.
And pretty soon, it's there.
You know it's all around.
It's right there,
and the People are right there.
That's the place Indians talk about.

And now,
they have a fence around the Coso Hot Springs.
We go up there, but they have a fence around.
They have a government fence all around Coso Hot Springs.
Since World War II, the Navy of the government
has a fence around that place.
The People go up there to talk with the hot springs,
to use the power, to keep ourselves well with,
but there is a fence with locks all around,
and we have to talk with the Navy people
so they can let us inside the fence to the hot springs.

We go up there to talk with the hot springs power
but the Navy tells us we have to talk to them.
We don't like it, to have to do that.

We don't want to talk to the government fence,
the government Navy.
That's the place the Indian people are talking about now.

For many years,
the People went up there.
Families from all over.
From Nevada, from Utah, from Arizona,
from north California, from south,
from all over, from anyplace.
Families have to travel by horses,
wagons, and now by cars, and walking.
We keep going up there,
for all this many years, we have to.
To keep talking to the power
of the power in the earth, we have to.
That's the Indian way.

We don't like to talk to the fence and the Navy
but for a while we will and pretty soon
we will talk to the hot springs power again.
That's the place Indians talk about.

                         Listen,
that's the way you hear.
Pretty soon, you can hear it,
coming far away
deep in the ground, deep down there coming,
the voice of the power coming,
closer and closer.
Listen, that's the way you hear it.
From the earth,
the moving power of the voice

and the People talking.
Praying, you know, singing soft too.

                              Hearing,
that's the way you listen.
The People talking,
telling the power to come to them
and pretty soon it will come.
It will come,
the moving power of the voice,
the moving power of the earth,
the moving power of the People.
That's the place Indian People talk about.

GEORGE BLUEEYES

Sacred Mountains

Díí Dził ahéénínilígíí
Nihi Bee Haz'áanii át'é.

    Sis Naajiní
    Tsoodził
    Dook'o'oosłíid
    Dibé Nitsaa
    Dził Ná'oodiłii
    Ch'óol'į́'í

Kót'éego éí nihá ályaa.
Éí nihighan át'é.

Sis Naajiní yoołgaii yee hadít'é.
Tsoodził dootł'izhii yee hadít'é.
Dook'o'oosłíid diichiłí yee hadít'é.
Dibé Nitsaa bááshzhinii yee hadít'é.

Dził Ná'oodiłii yódí yee hadít'é.
Ch'óol'į́'í nitł'iz yee hadít'é.

Ákót'éego nihá naazdá.
T'áá éí bíni' bik'ehgo
Yoo' dóó látsíní bee hadíníit'é.

Níléídę́ę́' ni' bitł'ááhdę́ę́' háát'i'.
Dził sinil áadi t'áá kót'éego
Nídahidiijaa'ii áádę́ę́' bił ha'azná,
T'áá íídą́ą́' dziłígíí ninádaas'nil.

Kodi dził ninádaas'nil.
Nahasdzáán ánályaa.
Yádiłhił ánályaa.
Hayoołkááł ánályaa.

Nahasdzáán nihimá.
Yádiłhił nihitaa'.
Jíhonaa'éí nihik'éé' diiłdíín.
Tł'éhonaa'éí dó'.
Éí bik'ehgo kééhwiit'í.

Níláhdę́ę́' hayoołkááł.
Hayoołkááł dine'é ádaaní,
    "Nídoohjeeh, nídoohjeeh!
    "Shitsóóké nídoohjeeh!"

Jíhonaa'éí t'áá ákót'éego hanáánádzih,
    "Nídoohjeeh, nídoohjeeh!
    "T'áadoo le'é baa naahkai.
    "Nidaałnish!
    "Hat'íí shíí ádaałééh, ádaałe'."

Ałné'é'áahgo ánáádí'niih,
    "K'ad nááda'ohdą́."

E'e'áahgo chahałheeł nihik'i náánéildoh,
    "Háádaałyį́į́h, háádaałyį́į́h, da'ołhosh."
Hááda'ayį́į́hgo yiłkááh.

Kót'éego éí bił hosiidlį́į́'.
Kót'éego éí bii' kééhwiit'į́.

Dził t'éí bee nihidziil.
Dził t'éí bee hat'íi da neiilyé.
Dził t'éí bee iidą́, bee iilghał.

Dził bileezh nideiijaah, Dah Nídiilyééh bidii'ní.
Binahjį' dibé, béégashii, łį́į́' da nidaakai.
Binahjį' naalyéhé, yódí da nidaajaah.
Bee yáti', bee tsohodizin.
Tsodizin bits'ą́ą́dóó deezt'i'.

—Tábąąhí Ts'ósí

Our Navajo Laws are represented by the
Sacred Mountains which surround us.

Sis Naajiní	Blanca Peak
Tsoodził	Mount Taylor
Dook'o'oosłííd	San Francisco Peaks
Dibé Nitsaa	Hesperus Peak
Dził Ná'oodiłii	Huerfano Mountain
Ch'óol'į́'í	Gobernador Knob

They were placed here for us.
We think of them as our home.

Blanca Peak is adorned with white shell.
Mount Taylor is adorned with turquoise.
San Francisco Peaks are adorned with abalone.
Hesperus Peak is adorned with jet.

Huerfano Mountain is dressed in
        precious fabrics,
While Governador Knob is clothed in
        sacred jewels.

This is how they sit for us.
We adorn ourselves just as they do,
With bracelets of turquoise,
And precious jewels about our necks.

The Sacred Mountains have always been
        where they are now.
They have been like that from the beginning.
They were like that in worlds before this.
They were brought up from the Underworld
And were put back in their respective places.

When the mountains were replaced,
Earth was made.
Sky was made.
Dawn was made.

Earth is Our Mother.
Sky is Our Father.
Sun gives us light.
Moon does the same.
All of these were made for us to live by.

The Dawn People say to us,
        "Get up, my grandchildren!
        "Rise! Do your work!
        "Do all the things that you must do!"

At noon the Sun tells us,
        "It's time to eat!"
And in the evening, when the Sun sets,
Darkness says to us,
        "Rest! Sleep, my grandchildren!"
Then Darkness blankets us,
And we rest until dawn.
This is how they have regulated our lives
        since the beginning.

These mountains and the land between them
Are the only things that keep us strong.
From them, and because of them we prosper.
It is because of them that we eat plants and good meat.

We carry soil from the Sacred Mountains in a
        prayer bundle that we call *dah nídiilyééh*.
Because of this bundle we gain sheep, horses,
        and cattle.
We gain possessions and things of value,
        turquoise, necklaces, and bracelets.
With this we speak, with this we pray.
This is where the prayers begin.

DANIEL LOPEZ

. . . .

Wi'ikam Do'ag

Wi'ikam Do'ag
Wi'ikam Do'ag
gan hu si s-ap masma an ke:k
heg da:m g huhugam 'o'odham an ki:kahim

Lonely Mountain

Lonely Mountain
Lonely Mountain
Over there it stands so finely
On top of this lonely mountain
    "the disappeared people" once lived.

FELIPE S. MOLINA

Sewailo Malichi

Aa sewailo malichi yewelu sika
    yo chikti yo sea
      huya aniwapo
        yeulu sika
sewailo malichi yewelu sika
    yo chikti yo sea
      huya aniwapo
        yeulu sikaaa

Aa sewailo malichi yewelu sika
    yo chikti yo sea
      huya aniwapo
        yeulu sika
sewailo malichi yewelu sika
    yo chikti yo sea
      huya aniwapo
        yeulu sikaaa

Ayamansu sewailo
    yo fayaliasu
      weyekai
        yeulu sika
sewailo malichi yewelu sika
    yo chikti yo sea
      huya aniwapo
        yeulu sikaaa

15

Flower-Covered Fawn

Aa flower-covered fawn went out,
   enchanted, from each enchanted flower
     wilderness world,
       he went out.
Flower-covered fawn went out,
   enchanted, from each enchanted flower
     wilderness world,
       he went out.

Aa flower-covered fawn went out,
   enchanted, from each enchanted flower
     wilderness world,
       he went out.
Flower-covered fawn went out,
   enchanted, from each enchanted flower
     wilderness world,
       he went out.

Over there, in the flower-covered
   enchanted opening,
     as he is walking,
       he went out.
Flower-covered fawn went out,
   enchanted, from each enchanted flower
     wilderness world,
       he went out.

This is always the first song of the *pahko*. In it we talk about *saila maaso*, little brother deer, as a young deer, a fawn. During the night of the *pahko*, he will grow up. In this song we talk about him coming out to walk around and to play in an enchanted opening in the flower world, his home. When I sing, my mind is always in the flower world. That is where I think the songs take place. There must be an opening in the wilderness over there in the flower world. The fawn comes out into that to dance and to play.

I learned this song from Miki Maaso. He always begins the first part of his songs with an "*aa*" to carry him into the song. So when I sing his songs, I do that too. *Chikti* means each. I am not sure just what it means in this song, but when I sing it I think about Don Jesús. He talked about *chikti huya,* meaning each and every tree and bush in the wilderness world. The fawn must go out from each and every part of the wilderness world.

DAN HANNA

. . . .

Medicine Song

Dan Hanna learned this song from Mark Hanna, a shaman. Although it
is a medicine song, it is not necessarily sung by a medicine man. It can
be sung by someone who is ill and wants to cure himself. Many people
had these personal medicine songs in the old days, and some people still
do. Like the medicine man's songs, a personal medicine song is received
through a dream from a spirit. The song goes into rich description of
Havasu Canyon. At the end, the song refers to some boulders which lie
in a certain place, which, when one lies down on them, absorb sickness.
The word *bay gjama*, which is translated as "an illness," is more correctly
either an illness or an accident, and really refers to a straying from the
rightful road, the development of a disharmony with nature—which is
what illness is defined to be.

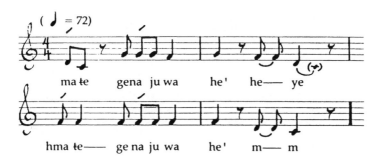

19

Singing		*Speaking*
Máte genájuwa	he′ heye	(′mat gnaajva)
Hmáte genájuwa	he′ mm	
Vá geyóvuwa	he′ heye	(va gyova)
Vá geyóvuwa	he′ heye	
′Áwe yuhwátiga	he′ heye	(′wii hwatga)
′Áwe yuhwátiga	he′ heyem	
Ñá oséemega	he′ heye	(ñaa seemga)
Ñá oséemega	he′ heye	
Ñá om gyájvga	he′ heye	(ñvgyajvga)
Ñá om vgyájevega	he′ hemm	
′áwam sigávoga	he′ heye	(′wa sgavoga)
′wámje sigávoga	he′ heyem	
Wé yiwáthuga	he′ heye	(′wii hwatega)
Wé yiwáthiga	he′ heye	
Ñá om mgyávoga	he′ mm	(nvgyajvga)
Thá giyóhuwa	he′ heye	(tha gyova)
Ñévo ñibúvguge	he′ heye	(ñvu ñbuvgge)
Hábag ñiyújuwa	he′ heye	(haabag nyuj)
Ñá guwíjuvuwo	he′ heyem	(na gwiijva)
Ñá guwíjuwo	he′ mm	
Hé ñiyúmowe	he′ heye	(ga vuñyum)
Gávo ńyúmowe	he′ heye	
′Máte ñuwíjuwa	he′ heye	(′mat ñwiijva)
Ñévo ñitúvume	he′ heye	

Singing		*Speaking*
Só 'ugwáthuga	he' heye	(suuwgwatga)
Vám jimísevga	he' hemm	
Ñó 'iyúhuwa	he' heye	(ña yuha)
Ñá 'iyúhuwa	he' heyem	
'Á giyúyuwo	he' heye	(ham s'ivtvga)
Hámes'e'ívtevga	he' heye	
'áme si'ívtevga	he' heye	(suuwgwatga)
Só'ogwátuwa	he' heyem	
'Ám buwámbuga	he' heye	(ham vwamvga)
Ñá 'iyúwuwa	he' heye	(ña yuha)
'Á gejúyiwo	he' heyem	(ha gyuuyo)
'Á 'amálega	he' heyem	(ha 'malga)
'Á 'amálega	he' heyem	
'Á gejúyiwo	he' heyem	
Gwáyve gwáyvuga	he' heye	(thgwayv
		thgwayvga)
Gwáyve gwáyvuga	he' heyem	
'Á gejúyiwo	he' heyem	(ha gyuuyo)
'Á gejúyiwo	he' heyem	
Má gwanóvjiga	he' heye	('mat gwanvjga)
Mát gwanóvjiga	he' eyem	
'Á gejúyiwo	he' heye	(sgwin sgwinga)
Máthgwinath-	he' heye	
gwínega		

Singing		*Speaking*
Máthgwinath-gwínega	he′ heye	(ña yuha)
Ñá iyúwawa	he′ mm	
Ñá ′iyúhuwa	he′ heya	(ha gbadga)
Háge ′abádiga	he′ heye	
Ágeyabádiga	he′ heyem	(ha javme)
Há ñijáwome	he′ heyem	
Ñévo jiháyviga	he′ heye	(ñvu jhayvga)
Ñá iyíwuwa	he′ heyem	(ña yuha)
′Ámesegwáthuga	he′ heye	(hamsgwathga)
Hámesegwáthega	he′ heye	
Shó′ogwáthuga	he′ heye	(suuwgwatga)
Shó′ogwáthuga	he′ heyem	
Há ñiyálowe	he′ heye	(ha ñyaala)
Há ñiyálowe	he′ heye	
Mágnognóvoga	he′ heye	(gnov gnovga)
Mágnognóvoga	he′ heye	
Ñá′iyúhuwa	he′ heye	(ña yuha)
Ñá′iyúhuwa	he′hmm	
Há ñiyálowe	he′ heye	(ha ñyaala)
Há jwáiga	he′ heye	(ha jwayga)
Ñévo jiqvújega	he′ heye	(ñvu jqayvjga)
Géjijávuwa	he′ heye	(gjjavva)
Vóñijávume	he′ heye	
Há′eñihájiva	he′ heye	(ha ñhajva)

Singing		*Speaking*
'Á jimhévgowa	he' heyem	(ha jmhevga)
Máte megɫávoge	he' heye	('mat mgɫavge)
'Ó ɫeyávoga	he' heye	(vu ɫyavge)
Thá thelávuma	he' heyem	(tha thlavm)
Ña 'iyúhuwa	he' heye	(ña yuha)
Ña 'iyúhuwa	he' heyem	
Thág ño'evó'oga	he' heye	(thag ñ'voga)
Thág ño'evó'oga	he' heyem	
Báyovgijámoha	he' heye	(bay gjama)
Báyogijámoha	he' heye	
Thá vuwámuga	he' heye	(thag vwamg)
Thá vuwámuga	he' heyem	
Gwéwe 'eswáduga	he' heye	(gwe 'swaadga)
Gwéwe 'eswáduga	he' heyem	
Ñá 'iyúhuwa	he' heye	(ña yuha)
Ñá 'iyúhuwa	he' heye	
'Ágwe simájuwa	he' heye	(gwe smaaje)
'Ágwe simájuwa	he' mm	
Bá qetheyévuwa	he' heye	('ba gthiyeva)
Bá qetheyévuwa	he' heye	
Vá'aluwíñuga	he' heye	(vlwiivga)
Vá'aluwíñuga	he'hmm	
Báyo gijámuha	he' heye	(bay gjama)
Báyo gijámuga	he' heye	
Há buwámuga	he' heye	(thag vwamg)
Há buwámuga	he' hmm	

Singing		*Speaking*
'Ágwe weswáduga	he' heye	(gwe 'swaadga)
'Ágwe weswáduga	he' heye	
'Ágwe 'asíñiga	he' heyem	(gwe 'siiñga)
'Ágwe 'asiñiga	he' heyem	
'Ate nemáguga	he' heye	('tnmagga)
'Ate nemáguga	he' heye	
Nó 'iyúhuwa	he' heye	(ña yuha)
Nó 'iyúhuwa	he' mm	
Thág ño'ovóga	he' heye	(thag ñ'vóga)
Thág ño'ovóga	he' heye	
Thám jovibájuga	he' heyem	(tham jo jbajga)
Thám jo wibájuga	he' heye	
Mátoódwova	he' heye	('mat t'odva)
Mátoódwova	he' mm	
Gwé ñihátowa	he' heye	(gwe ñhat)
Gwé ñihátowa	he' heye	
Ñó 'uwávowo	he' heye	(ñowavo)
Ño'uwávowo	he' heyem	
Ñwá 'ajóqowa	he' heyem	(ñwa 'joq)
Jóqa havítega	he' heyem	('joq hvitga)
Ñabiñáboga	he' heye	(ñab ñabga)
Vú 'ayóhowa	he' heye	(vu gyoha)
Gwé ñihátove	he' heye	(gwe ñhat)
Thám jejebúvuvga	he' heye	(tham jjbugvga)
Ñó 'iyúhuwa	he' heye	(ña yuha)
Ñó 'iyúhuwa	he' heyem	

Singing		Speaking
Thág ño'evówoga	he' heye	(thag ñ'voga)
Thág ño'evówoga	he' heyem	
Yá hawíniga	he' heye	(siihwinga)
Yá hawíniga	he' hmm	
'Áwe gewéyiwo	he' heye	('wii gweeyi)
'Áwe gewéyiwo	he' heyem	
'Áwe gethíltewa	he' heye	('wii gthiltva)
Ña'usémuga	he' heye	(ñaa seemga)
'Ó ñibóvuvga	he' heyem	(vu ñbuvvga)
Hábav ñiyújuwa	he' heyem	(haabag ñyuj)
'Ágwe ñigethá-temwa	he' heye	(gwe ñgthaajme)
Ñá geyóhuwa	he' heye	(ñgyoha)
Gá geyóhowa	he' heyem	(gwe ñhaŧa)
Gwé'e ñiháŧowa	he' heye	
Únihájuve	he' heye	(vu ñhajva)
Gá geyóhowa	he' hemm	(ga gyoha)
'Áwe gethílŧega	he' heye	('wii gthilŧga)
Ñá vusémuga	he' heyem	(ñaa seemga)
Ñam gyávuga	he' heye	(ñvgyávga)
Thá thiyóvuwa	he' heye	(tha gyova)
Ñívu vetóvume	he' heyem	(ñvu vtuvme)
Gwé'e ñihátuwa	he'mm	(gwe ñhata)
Ñóviñájuwo	he' heye	(ññáaje)
Ñóviñájuwo	he' heye	

Singing		*Speaking*
'Ágwe gethávuga	he' heye	(gwe gthavga)
'Ágwe gethávuga	he' heyem	
Ó eye'óyvuga	he' heye	(vu ɫs'uuyvga)
Májyo yi'úyvuga	he' heye	
Vógse vuwávuga	he' heyem	(buge vwavga)
Vógse vuwávuga	he' heyem	
Tháge yóvuwa	he' heye	(vá gyóva)
Ñó 'iyúhuwa	he' heye	(ñá 'yúha)
Ág ño'uvówuga	he' heye	(thag ñyovga)
Jégamímowa	he'mm	(jgmimo)
'Áwe ñihwáɫoga	he' heye	('wii hwaɫog)
Jé gamímoga	he' eye	
Vú giyóvume	he' heyem	(vu gyovme)
Amqe ghmimoga	hm' hmm	
'Áse yehwáɫega	he' heye	
Míñabeñáboga	he' heye	(vñab ñabga)
Ó giyóvume	he' heye	
Ñáj ivóguwa	he' heyem	(ñaj voga)
'Á'iyámoga	he' heye	('yaamga)
Ñá'ji yúwuga	he' heyem	(ñaj yuhga)
'Áwe huhwáɫega	he' heyem	('wii hwaɫga)
Ñá 'usémega	he' heyem	(ñaa seemga)
Ñá em 'ugyávuga	he' heye	(ñvgyajvga)
Vú giyówuwa	he' heye	(vu gyova)
Ñóm ñibóvuge	he'mm	(nvu vbuvge)
'Áwe yihwáɫega	he'eche	('wii hwaɫga)

Singing   *Speaking*
Óhwináloga   he′ heye   (onalga)
Thá vuséemuga   he′mm   (tha vseemga)

Thá vuséemuga   he′ heye
Thági yóthuwa   he′eye   (tha gyova)

′Áwovethátevemo   he′ heye   (vthatvmo)
Ágiyóhuwa   he′ heye

Yá ′iyíñuwa   he′ heye   (ya ′yiiñu)
Yá ′iyíñuwa   he′ heye

The land we were given
The land we were given

It is right here
It is right here

Red rock
Red rock

Streaked with brown
Streaked with brown

Shooting up high
Shooting up high

All around our home
All around our home

Red rock
Red rock

Shooting up high
It is right here

Down at the source
A spring will always be there

It is ours
It is ours

Since a long time ago
Since a long time ago

In the land that is ours
Moving right down the center

Bright blue-green
There moves a line

This is what I'm thinking
This is what I'm thinking

At the edge of the water
Cattails appear

Cattails appear
Bright blue-green

All around the water
This is what I'm thinking

At the edge of the water
Water foam forming

Water foam forming
At the edge of the water

Swirl, swirling
Swirl, swirling

At the edge of the water
At the edge of the water

Silt layers forming
Silt layers forming

At the edge of the water
Ripple, rippling

Ripple, rippling
This is what I'm thinking

This is what I'm thinking
Water-walking beetles

Water-walking beetles
On top of the water

Spreading out
This is what I'm thinking

Water grasses growing
Water grasses growing

Bright blue-green
Bright blue-green

Under the water
Under the water

Wave, waving
Wave, waving

This is what I'm thinking
This is what I'm thinking

Under the water
Water pebbles

Tiny little ones
Spreading out over them

Spreading out over them
Our drinking water

The water is gliding
Toward the north

On in that direction
And then it is gone

This is what I'm thinking
This is what I'm thinking

Here we arrive
Here we arrive

An illness
An illness

I sit down
I sit down

I sing myself a song
I sing myself a song

This is what I'm thinking
This is what I'm thinking

A medicine spirit
A medicine spirit

A shaman
A shaman

I am the same as him
I am the same as him

An illness
An illness

I sit down
I sit down

I sing myself a song
I sing myself a song

The things I have named
The things I have named

I leave them behind
I leave them behind

This is what I'm thinking
This is what I'm thinking

There we arrive
There we arrive

We are leaving the canyon
We are leaving the canyon

Out on the rim
Out on the rim

Horses that are mine
Horses that are mine

The place where they roam
The place where they roam

Is there at the junipers
Where the junipers are straight

And low and low
They are right here

Horses that are mine
Are gathered right there.

This is what I'm thinking
This is what I'm thinking

Here we arrive
Here we arrive

We swing back
We swing back

Descending the rocks again
Descending the rocks again

White rock
Streaked with brown

Down at the source
A spring will always be there

The spring that heals
It is right there

It is right there
Horses that are mine

They drink the water
That is right there

White rock
Streaked with brown

Shooting up high
It is right there

Moving down the center
Horses that are mine

There is their trail
There is their trail

The color of dust
The color of dust

Zig-zagging
Zig-zagging

It leads to the source
It leads to the source

It is right here
This is what I'm thinking

Here we arrive
Down in the canyon

Red rocks
Down in the canyon

They are right here
Down in the canyon

Red rocks
Low and low

They are right here
Here I walk

I go alone
This is what I'm thinking

Red rocks
Streaked with brown

Shooting up high
It is right here

Down at the source
Red rocks

Boulders they are
Streaked with brown

Streaked with brown
They are right here

Where my illness is absorbed
It is right here

This is what I will
This is what I will

Transcribed and translated by Leanne Hinton

RALPH CAMERON

. . . .

'inyamat 'inychxa 'inychaviish

'inyamat thany xumarxaayly 'iyuuk vinyathiim,
xaxan thash palyk shakamp kovark.
vii vakava'osh thash waly noqampamak chaxotilyaviik xmiik
vataym, mat nyim'oyuuvk viiva'oshk.
mat nyixamev thash kwilyshawk.
uuva'awsh as'uulyik taklasham, miyuum chaxotilyaviik
mapis aanya walyviimak.
thany 'iyuuk vinyav'awm, nyip 'iyem'athoy thash.
xa'ash kushlyuuvevak pamm shmaanysh ashpashm miyuuk.
aanya 'ilyviitk 'avtik
   'uuva'otintiyuum
'esa 'etik.
'ayuush palyik aampsa 'etik.
walynyuupaymxaayk.
xa kovtash thash 'inyaashpak asily shathaakalyskiitk.
vii koxshamenysh viiva'oshxaaysa 'etik.
yaa kovevak xa kovatash vishathaakxaayk.
thany 'iyoovk vinyava'ok.
piipaa thash uuva'ok
   'uuva'otintiyuum
'esa 'etik. 'ayuu kw'empa 'athawishintiyuum
'esa 'etik.

piipaa nyikur thash vathuu vathiik thany thawshik uuva'ak
vinyathiik thany
   'ilyavetntiyuum

Transcription by Lynn Gordon

My Land, My Water, My Mountains

When I was young, I saw my land as I grew up.
The rivers were many and without price.
The mountains there had not been touched.
They were beautiful, tall and big and they stood out.
The land I was born on was clean.
The rain washed it and purified it.
You saw it and it was very good.
Now it is not like that.
I see this.
This is my tradition.
A tree half fallen down with its roots showing—I feel
I am like that,
   I say we will stand again.
I see many things are left that haven't vanished yet.
The great lakes of the East are still there.
The tall mountains are still there.
The great rivers of the Northwest still exist.
We see this.
The people will walk again, I say.
We will again have the truth.
Our forefathers did this; they took this; they progressed up until now.
   I say we can do this too.

LANCE HENSON

Glimpse of Home

somewhere behind your eyes
the house of your childhood appears

deep in your blood
you have said the words again
they walk from you into the silence
of a snowy field

the cry of a bird will lead the dark away
from itself

toward dawn
his wings will dance the moon
home

GEORGIANA VALOYCE-SANCHEZ

Fat of the Land

Walking to public school
beyond the housing project compound
I would ponder the "fat
of the land"
What it meant
Why my folks always talked
about it

When there was nothing left to eat
but beans   Steinbeck
would appear at our table
blowing smoke rings with his big
cigar and he'd lean back in our
rickety kitchen chair and talk
about the "fat
of the land"

When I got older with babies and
two cars in my suburban garage
my folks went back home
to Indian land
Reservation   rocks broken bottle glass
an old shack in the foothills
of the San Gorgonio's

and I asked them
is this it Is this
It?
Where's the fat?
And my father would lean back against
a scrawny birch   blow smoke rings
with his clay pipe   and smile

I had to admit
the handful of pale pink strawberries
he had coaxed from the stony ground
were the   sweetest
I had ever tasted
and there was no denying
the singing that took place
when my mother and father knelt
to pat the earth
beneath the bare peach tree

LINDA HOGAN

Water Rising

We rose up from the rocks
like the night a mineral spring
broke earth, a fresh wound
where we were sitting
and the geese flying so close
their air brushed our shoulders.
Small signs of the world
passing its own way.

I am just lungs, heart
and skin
trying to understand
a world going to rest,
your white hair,
the bruises beneath your skin.

We rose up from the same land
like clouds that move away,
the small deer that pass this way
and are gone,
and the water we drank
tasting iron, of blood.

There is magic when water opens
the walls of rock

like they are shells,
when it reaches the end of its journey
and finds itself waking
in another strange place.

Tonight when I speak of water,
I don't mean the big oceans
rocking themselves, but water
moving place to place
underground, small veins
finding their way to sunlight
where they rupture.

And while I say this
the signs are still coming,
a leaf is detaching itself from a tree
and falling, a last breath.
Night is growing darker
and geese, the geese
once again fly past the old route.
The magnetic springs
run smooth
the bones of the dead.
They hold our feet
and let us dance away
forever from the dark body.

RAMONA WILSON

December on the Coast

As I sleep the Grey Whales
swim and blow a smell of green and sea
into the moon-cold air.
They do not sleep, they court
and play even as they pull south
to the lagoons and sky
some have never seen.

All things fall away
before their intentness
their bulk rising like prophecy,
like dreams that begin
the same way, time after time.
They have no count
of miles or years
but answer to a memory
that is its own need.

I turn over with a dream of sun
turning my sleep like waves.
I wake restless into a day
murmuring of migrations.

ELIZABETH WOODY

. . . .

In Memory of Crossing the Columbia

CONCEPTION
My board and blanket were Navajo,
but my bed is inside the River.
In the beads of remembrance,
I am her body in my father's hands.
She gave me her eyes
and the warmth of basalt.
The vertebrae of her back,
my breastplate, the sturdy
belly of mountainside.

"Pahtu." he whispered in her language.
She is the mountain of change.
She is the mountain of women
who have lain as volcanoes
before men.

Red, as the woman much loved,
she twisted like silvery chinook
beyond his reach.

Dancing the Woman-Salmon dance,
there is not much time to waste.

WENDY ROSE

The Endangered Roots of a Person

I remember lying awake
in a Phoenix motel. Like that
I remember coming apart accidentally
like an isolated hunk of campfire soot
cornered by time into a cave.
I live even now
in an archaeological way.

    Becoming strong on this earth is a lesson
    in not floating, in becoming less transparent,
    in becoming an animal shape against the sky.

We were born
to lose our eyes in the Sun Dance
and send out lengths of fishline
for the clouds, reel them in
and smooth away all the droughts
of the world.

    Sometimes Medicine People shake their hands
    over you and it is this; to drop your bones
    into the sand, to view yourself
    bursting through the city
    like a brown flash flood.
    The healing of the roots

is that thunderhead-reeling;
they change and pale
but they are not in danger now.

That same morning
I went for coffee down the street
and held it, blowing dreams
through the steam, watching silver words
bead up on my skin. The Hand-trembler said
I belong here. I fit in this world
as the red porcelain mug
merges in the heat of my hand.

On some future dig
they'll find me like this
uncovered where I knelt
piecing together the flesh
that was scattered in the mesa wind
at my twisted-twin birth.

JOY HARJO

My house is the red earth; it could be the center of the world. I've heard New York, Paris, or Tokyo called the center of the world, but I say it is magnificently humble. You could drive by and miss it. Radio waves can obscure it. Words cannot construct it, for there are some sounds left to sacred wordless form. For instance, that fool crow, picking through trash near the corral, understands the center of the world as greasy scraps of fat. Just ask him. He doesn't have to say that the earth has turned scarlet through fierce belief, after centuries of heartbreak and laughter—he perches on the blue bowl of the sky, and laughs.

N. SCOTT MOMADAY

. . . .

From My Home of Jemez

It happened that a teaching job opened up at the Cañoncito Day School
on the Navajo reservation between Albuquerque and Gallup, and my
mother decided to take it. Sooner or later there would be two positions
somewhere, my mother was assured, and my father and I would join
her. And so it came about, sooner than could have been expected. In a
matter of days my parents were offered the two-teacher day school at
Jemez Pueblo, some fifty miles north and west of Albuquerque, due west
of Santa Fe, in the canyon country beneath the Jemez Mountains. None
of us had ever been there before. My mother went there directly from
Cañoncito, and my father and I collected our things and set out from
Hobbs with a man whom my father had hired to move us in his truck.
That was in September, 1946. We arrived late at night, having got lost
and gone nearly to Cuba, New Mexico, on the Farmington road. I can
still see that dirt and gravel road in the light of the headlamps, white,
with the black night on either side, the blue, black-dotted dunes in the
moonlight beyond, and the bright stars. Rabbits and coyotes crossed the
road. There was no pavement then on our way beyond Bernalillo, and
for the last thirty miles or so the little truck bounced and rattled into the
wild country. I could remember having, years before, when I was small,
driven with my father across Snake Flats, on the Navajo. In heavy rain
or snow the road was impassable, and we had had to wait until late at
night, when it was frozen hard, in order to drive upon it.

The next morning I woke up, and there was a great excitement in
me, as if something strange and wonderful had happened in the night:

I had somehow got myself deep into the world, deeper than ever before. Perhaps I really expected nothing, and so I could not have been disappointed, but I do not believe that. Anyway, no expectation could possibly have been equal to the brilliance and exhilaration of that autumn New Mexican morning. Outside I caught my breath on the cold, delicious air of the Jemez Valley, lying out at six thousand feet. Around me were all the colors of the earth that I have ever seen. As I think back to that morning, there comes to my mind a sentence in Isak Dinesen: "In the highlands you woke up in the morning and thought: Here I am, where I ought to be."

The valley slopes down from north to south, and the pueblo lies down in the depth of it, on the east bank of the shallow Jemez River. Some four miles to the north is the little settlement of Cañon, nestled in sheer formations of red rock, and beyond is the long, deep San Diego Canyon, rising sharply up to the dark-timbered walls of the Jemez Range, to the Valle Grande, which is the largest caldera in the world, and to the summit above eleven thousand feet, from which you can look across the distance eastward to the Sangre de Cristos. Five miles to the south is the village of San Ysidro, where the valley loses its definition and the earth fans out in wide reaches of white, semi-arid plains. The junction at San Ysidro is as close as you can come to Jemez Pueblo in a Trailways bus; State Road 44 runs south and east to Bernalillo, north and west to Cuba, Bloomfield, and Farmington, near my old home of Shiprock. The east side of the valley is a long blue mesa, which from the pueblo seems far away, and in my years there I never covered the whole distance between, though I rode around for a thousand miles, it may be, on horseback. The conformation of that mesa is the rule of a solar calendar; for as long as anyone knows the Jemez people have lived their lives according to the ranging of the sun as it appears every day on that long, level skyline. Closer on the west, across the river, the valley is sharp-edged, given up abruptly to a high, broken wall—to walls beyond walls—of many colors. There is the red mesa upon which are still to be found the ancient ruins of Zia, there the white sandstone cliffs in which is carved the old sacred cave of the Jemez Snake Clan, and there are pink and purple hills, ascending to the lone blue mountain in the northwest, where there are bears and mountain lions as well as deer and where once, in living memory, there were wolves.

The character of the landscape changed from hour to hour in the day, and from day to day, season to season. Nothing there of the earth could be taken for granted; you felt that Creation was going on in your sight. You see things in the high air that you do not see farther down in the lowlands. In the plains you can see farther than you have ever seen, and that is to gain a great freedom. But in the high country all objects bear upon you, and you touch hard upon the earth. The air of the mountains is itself an element in which vision is made acute; eagles bear me out. From my home of Jemez I could see the huge, billowing clouds above the Valle Grande, how, even motionless, they drew close upon me and merged with my life.

REFUGIO SAVALA

Growth: Merging Labor and Love

How things are natural in the wild
When the flowers, streams and the light
And the trees offer the shade so mild,
And protect the feeble bird aflight
Like the mother's tender love for a child,
Add to pleasure the most sensual delight.

After my father had been away six months, there was a stepfather for us
three children. With our new father we got a new sister named Eloisa,
and she claimed she got a mother, a sister, and us two brothers. Our new
father was not a railroad man. Best of all, he was not a drinking man. He
was a big man, a heavy-set six-footer who worked adobes by contract.
In this work, he made men of us two boys. He ran the molder for four
bricks of prepared mud, while my brother Fernando ran the wheelbar-
row. I would prepare the mud with straw and dung. We got thirty dollars
for a thousand bricks. In a week's work we also put time into laying out
the adobes for the sun to dry them and into stacking them for delivery.

Then the time came for our father to work out of town up on Cañada
del Oro, which is on the west end of the Catalina mountain range. He
was given a big green wagon with a horse team to take the whole family,
and we loaded all our possessions and headed up north toward the Cata-
linas. We came to a park, the last grocery store, then crossed Rillito
River. No bridge was put up in those days, so we went across the river,
but there was no water, so the crossing was on the sandy riverbed. Then

we came up to the top of the hill. Then we reached Oracle Junction, and taking the road to the right, we started into Llano Toro [Bull's Plain], a cholla forest with cattle roaming. They were decorated with cactus spines all over, even their faces. Our father knew the desert, and when we came to a ranch at Toro Cañada creek, he told us that it was the old post where the stagecoach took relief coming into town. In those days ore from the mining camps was hauled by mule train, and these we saw in town. They stopped for the mules to drink at the city water trough.

Our destination was reached when we came to Rancho Samaniego. The Cañada del Oro was flowing with a torrent of clear water, very beautiful. Our father was not working Sundays, so he told us about the way he came to Arizona. He crossed from Mexico at Douglas, going through Cochise County to Willcox on to Bowie and on to Safford, San Carlos, and Globe.

In our camp, we had a large tent to live in. The foreman had a Mexican wife, so he could talk Spanish. They lived in a building made of lumber. Our father told us we did not have to work, so we became again two playmates, but the ranch foreman's wife soon put us to work with her own boys as *wok bake'om* [walking cowboys], herding the cows to the corral early in the morning for milking. We drank much milk every morning as *wok bake'om*, and we had dinner with the foreman's family at noon. What we liked very much was the *kuahada* [cottage cheese]. This is the cheese which has not been put in the molder. This woman made the molders so big that when the cheese came out, it was about the size of a *tampaleo kubahi* [Pascola drum].

Every day after being *wok bake'om*, we had all day to go places. Going upstream, we found a good swimming hole. This was one pastime for us, and so was walking into the canyon to see the spring water flowing into the main stream. This canyon was deep, the walls on both sides solid rock. In the solid rock bottom, we found little bowls made by hand by the Indians of this river, for the purpose of catching rain water to drink when water was scarce. My father called them *tesa akim* in Yaqui.

Truly, we were enjoying ourselves here more than in town.

The study of Cañada del Oro was of much profit to me. I learned all about ranch life since both my parents had great experience. I learned the Yaqui names of plants and fowls and about taking bees for wild honey. The *siba wikit*, cliff bird, is a day bird and sings at dawn. *Kauru-akte'a*, a night bird, sings all night.

The perfume flower plant is the Spanish *vinodama* [*kuka* in Yaqui]. You can sense the perfume from a long distance. My father told me how the Indians knew God by this perfume.

Before the white man, the Yaquis saw God in this creation. They saw him in the firmament's heavenly bodies, his spirit in the perfume of the *sewam* [flowers]. They would say, "*Wame'e bwere chokim iefforing* [Go the planets when our earth is suspended], For there is nothing covered that shall not be revealed" (Matthew 10:26). The Yaquis, not having any Bible study, many times tell whole chapters of the Gospel, as my own father gave me the definition of the fifth commandment: "Thou shalt not kill; do not be unjust, unkind. Do not take little animals to be a nuisance. They are made to be with us. Rather be a life saver. If you see a fly in a bucket of water trying to save itself, stick your finger in the water, let it crowd up, and snap it into the air. Here you save one life as precious to God as yours."

My father also told me of an aged Pascola Dancer who gave, in a fiesta closing sermon, a verse from the seventh chapter of Matthew, "Enter ye in at the strait gate" (Matt. 7:13). In telling the deceitfulness of the broad road he said, "But the road to heaven is a narrow footpath in the ground, narrow for not being much in use, for there be few that find it." The name of this Pascola Dancer was *Wahu Chahi* [Falcon], and the sermon was given at Mesquitalito in Tucson.

Another story he told was of Peo, which means Pedro. Peo was a big liar and deceiver all over the eight villages of the Río Yaqui. One day a priest came riding a mule. He met Peo and asked him to fool him as he had heard. Peo said, "Father, I have to get my book with which I do my tricks to deceive people, but wait here and I'll go get it." The priest said, "Take my mule and go get the book." So Peo took the mule but did not return to the priest again. This man told his lies so realistically, he even fooled himself. He told one person in Guaymas that a whale was lying on the sand at the seashore. The word was passed all over town. He saw the people running to see the whale, and when he was told about it, he started running also to see it. When he arrived where the people were, there was no whale. There was confusion, and people asked who had said there was one. Peo himself was asking the same question.

All these stories were told in Yaqui by my father in Cañada del Oro. Then the time came for us to go back to town. We had to go home because my mother was pregnant and also because the work was finished. When my father was dismissed, he was given the same green wagon and horses. I was exceedingly sorry to leave, but we said goodbye to our ranch friends: *"Adiós, hasta la otra visita con el favor de Dios."*

When we pulled out of the canyon, we were again on the Llano Toro. Up here we saw the canal which brought water by force of gravity from up the river so that Llano Toro was made a farmland. They raised wheat and barley. It was wonderful, for the river water was turned up on the hills without a dam. We were on the same route as we came on, passing the *cuesta* [hill] and the old post. Then we started going around the west end of the Catalina Mountains. The huge mountains seemed to be standing at the same distance, but Tucson became visible. There was no hurry, and my father never used the whip on the horses because they went fast enough at ease until we arrived home. We caused a sensation with the neighbor kids. They asked me if we saw genuine Indians, and we told them that we were the genuine Indians up there.

NORA NARANJO-MORSE

Ta

I asked about success
    how was I to measure it,
    struggling in
    two worlds,
      between Pueblo tradition
      and modern values.
    Keeping on course,
     a balance
     of who I am
        and wish to become.
Ta took his time answering.
    I thought maybe
     he hadn't heard,
     or worse,
     not listened.
    Waiting
     I noticed,
     how time
     had tailored my father
     into an old man
     wrinkled
       and halting.
    Finally,
     with clear

thoughtful words,
my father spoke:
"Navi a yu,
hi wu na mang,
uvi aa yaa,
uvi seng,
da hihchan po o.
Navi a yu,
hi wodi kwee un muu,
oe to jan be,
hi wo na mang,
sa wo na mang."
"My daughter,
it is going well,
your children,
your husband,
are happy.
My daughter,
you are a good woman,
listen,
it is going well,
it goes in beauty."
Simple
words,
    reminding me,
    success
    is not only
    respecting tradition
    or balancing
    modern values.
    It is the appreciation
    of life's basic gifts,   ·

weaving
into the whole
of who you are
and who you can become.
Ta sat under the Elm,
  drifting to sleep
      his hand in mine.

OFELIA ZEPEDA

Pulling Down the Clouds

Ñ-ku'ipaḍkaj 'ant 'an o 'ols g cewagĭ.
With my harvesting stick I will hook the clouds.
Nt o 'i-wannio k o 'i-huḍiñ g cewagĭ.
With my harvesting stick I will pull down the clouds.
Ñ-ku'ipaḍkaj 'ant o 'i-siho g cewagĭ.
With my harvesting stick I will stir the clouds.

With dreams of a distant noise disturbing his sleep,
the smell of dirt, wet, for the first time in what seemed
like months.
The change in the molecules is sudden, they enter
the nasal cavity.
He contemplates the smell, what is that smell?
It is rain.
Rain somewhere out in the desert.
Comforted in this knowledge he turns over
and continues his sleep,
dreams of women with harvesting sticks
raised toward the sky.

LUCI TAPAHONSO

The Motion of Songs Rising

The October night is warm and clear.
We are standing on a small hill and in all directions,
around us, the flat land listens to the songs rising.
The holy ones are here dancing.
The Yeis are here.

In the west, Shiprock looms above the desert.
Tsé bit'a'í, old bird-shaped rock. She watches us.
Tsé bit'a'í, our mother who brought the people here on her back.
Our refuge from the floods long ago. It was worlds and centuries ago
yet she remains here. Nihimá, our mother.

This is the center of the night
and right in front of us, the holy ones dance.
They dance, surrounded by hundreds of Navajos.
                         Diné t'óó àhayóí.
                         Diné t'óó àhayóí.
We listen and watch the holy ones dance.
                         Yeibicheii.
                         Yeibicheii.
                         Grandfather of the holy ones.

They dance, moving back and forth.
Their bodies are covered with white clay
and they wave evergreen branches.

They wear hides of varying colors,
their coyote tails swinging as they sway back and forth.
All of them dancing ancient steps.
They dance precise steps, our own emergence onto this land.

They dance again, the formation of this world.
They dance for us now—one precise swaying motion.
They dance back and forth, back and forth.
As they are singing, we watch ourselves recreated.

Éí áłts'íísígíí shił nizhóní. The little clown must be about six years old.
He skips lightly about waving his branches around. He teases people in
the audience, tickling their faces if they look too serious or too sleepy.
At the beginning of each dance, when the woman walks by to bless the
Yeis, he runs from her. Finally, after the third time, she sprinkles him
with corn pollen and he skips off happily. 'éí shił nizhóní.

The Yeis are dancing again, each step, our own strong bodies.
They are dancing the same dance, thousand of years old. They are here
for us now, grateful for another harvest and our own good health.
>The roasted corn I had this morning was fresh,
>cooked all night and taken out of the ground this
>morning. It was steamed and browned just right.

They are dancing and in the motion of songs rising,
our breathing becomes the morning moonlit air.
The fires are burning below as always.
>We are restored.
>We are restored.

CARTER REVARD

An Eagle Nation

For the Camp/Jump brigades

You see, I remember this little Ponca woman
who turned her back to the wall and placed her palms
up over her shoulders flat on the wall
and bent over backwards and walked her hands down the wall
and placed them flat on the floor behind her back—that's
how limber she was, Aunt Jewell,
when I was a boy.
And FAST! you wouldn't BELIEVE how she could sprint:
when an Osage couple married, they would ask Aunt Jewell
to run for the horses for them.
Now she's the eldest in her clan, but still the fastest
to bring the right word, Ponca or English, sacred or
profane, whatever's needed to survive she brings it, sometimes in
a wheelchair, since her heart
alarms the doctors now and then.
So one bright day we loaded
the wheelchair, and ourselves, and lots of chicken
barbecued and picnic stuff
into our cars and zoomed away
from Ponca City and White Eagle, *Southward Ho!*
To the Zoo, we said, the Oke City Zoo—we'd picnic there!
Grandchildren, see, they love the zoo,
and has she got GRANDchildren? well, maybe

one of her children knows how many, the rest of us
stopped counting years ago, so there were quite a few
with serious thoughts of chicken barbecue and we all rolled in
to the Zoo and parked, and we walked, and scrambled, and rolled,
we scuttled and sprinted, we used up all the verbs
in English, she'd have to get those Ponca words
to tell you how we made our way,
but somehow we ALL of us got in, and found
the picnic tables, and we feasted there and laughed
until it was time to inspect the premises, to see just what
the children of Columbus had prepared for us.
Snow leopards and black jaguars, seals and dolphins, monkeys and
baboons, the elephants and tigers looked away
thinking of Africa, of Rome, oceans, dinnertime, whatever—
and as for us, we went in all directions,
grandchildren rolled and bounced like marbles up and down
the curving asphalt ways, played hide and seek, called me to look
at camels maybe. And then we were all
getting tired and trying to reassemble, when Casey
came striding back to where we were wheeling Aunt Jewell
and said "Mom,
there's this eagle over here you should see,"
and we could tell it mattered. So we wheeled along
to this cage set off to itself with a bald eagle sitting,
eyes closed and statue-still,
on the higher perch inside, and there was a couple
standing up next to the cage and trying
to get its attention.
A nice white couple, youngish, the man
neatly mustached and balding, the woman
white-bloused and blondish: the man clapped hands
and clicked his tongue and squeaked, and whistled. The eagle

was motionless. Casey wheeled Aunt Jewell
a little to the side. The man stopped making noises.
He and the woman looked at each other, then at us, and
looked away.
There was a placard on the cage's side that said:
This bald eagle was found wounded, and
although its life was saved, it will never fly again,
so it is given this cage to itself.
Please do not feed him.
Aunt Jewell, from her wheelchair, spoke in Ponca to him,
so quietly that I could hardly hear
the sentences she spoke.
Since I know only
a few words of Ponca, I can't be sure
what she said or asked, but I caught the word
Kahgay:
Brother, she said.
The eagle opened his eyes and turned his head.
She said something else. He partly opened his beak
and crouched and looked head-on toward her,
and made a low shrill sound.
The white couple were kind of dazed, and so was I.
I knew she was saying good things for us.
I knew he'd pass them on.
She talked a little more, apologizing
for all of us, I think.
She put one hand up to her eyes and closed them for a while
till Casey handed her a handkerchief,
and she wiped her eyes.
"I guess we're 'bout ready to go now," Aunt Jewell said,
so we wheeled along back to the car, and we gathered all
the clan and climbed aboard

and drove from the Zoo downtown to where
the huge *Red Earth* powwow was going on, because
her grandson Wesley, Mikasi, was dancing there.
We hadn't thought Aunt Jewell's heart
was up to Zoo and Powwow in one day, but as usual she
knew better. They CHARGED ADMISSION, and that really
outraged my Ponca folks, for whom
a powwow should be free. Worse than that,
the contest DANCERS had to pay a fee.
"That's not our way," Aunt Jewell said.
But once inside we found our way,
wheelchair and all, up to the higher tiers,
where we and thousands of Indian people looked down
to the huge Arena floor where twelve drums
thundered and fourteen hundred dancers spun and eddied round,
and dancing in his wolfskin there
was Mikasi where Casey pointed, and we saw
his Grampa Paul Roughface gliding
with that eagle's calm he has,
and I saw how happy Casey and Mike were then
that their eldest son was dancing down there, and I felt
what the drum did for Aunt Jewell's heart and ours, and she told us
of seventy years ago when she was a little girl and her folks
would load the wagons up there in White Eagle and go
and ford the Arkansas into the Osage country and drive all day
and camp at night on the prairie and then drive on
to the Grayhorse Osage Dances, or those in Pawhuska even.
I remembered how Uncle Woody Camp had told me
of going to the Osage dances later and seeing her
for the first time and asking:
"Who IS that beautiful Ponca girl over there?"
and someone said,

"Oh that's McDonald's girl,"
and they met that way.
And he and Uncle Dwain would tell
of the covered wagon in which they rode,
my Irish and Scotch-Irish mother's folks, from Missouri out
to the Kansas wheat harvest, and then on down
to the Osage Reservation in Oklahoma, where mules were needed,
and our grandfather hauled the bricks to build
the oil-boom Agency town of Pawhuska, where the million-dollar
lease sales, and the Osage Dances, were held.
So I was thinking how the eagles soared,
in their long migration flights, over all these places,
how they looked down on the wagons moving
westward from Missouri, eastward from Ponca lands
to meet in Pawhuska, how all the circles
had brought us into this Oklahoma time and what
had passed between cage and wheelchair before
we mounted up to view on this huge alien floor the long-ago drum
in its swirling rainbow of feathers and
bells and moccasins lifting up here
the songs and prayers from long before cars or wagons,
and how it all has changed and the ways are strange but
the voices still
are singing, the drum-heart
still beating here, so whatever the placards on
their iron cages may have to say, we the people,
as Aunt Jewell and Sun Dancers say,
are an EAGLE NATION, now.

LARRY EVERS

. . . .

Sun Tracks: A Brief History and Checklist

In January 1971, three Navajo students from the University of Arizona—Carol Kirk, Orville McKinley, and David Jackson—gave a public program on "the life of the contemporary Indian" at the Tucson Public Library. Advertising suggests that the program responded to the rising tide of public interest in American Indians. In the way the students approached the Tucson Public Library presentation they demonstrated their engagement with the local, regional, and national Indian movements of their time. They showed slides of living conditions on the Navajo reservation, of a demonstration protesting the exploitation of Indians at the Gallup Ceremonial, and of the Indian takeover of Alcatraz Island in California. It was at the end of this discussion that they chose to announce plans for a new "American Indian literary quarterly" that Carol Kirk would edit. (*Arizona Daily Star*, Jan. 17, 1971.)

Support for the students' plans at the University of Arizona came from many people. An important early patron was Dr. Edward P. Dozier, a Tewa Indian from Santa Clara Pueblo, cultural anthropologist, and professor of anthropology at the University of Arizona from 1964 until his too-early death in 1971. Dr. Dozier worked hard during his years at the University of Arizona to found an American Indian studies program and to attract and retain Indian students at the university. He was active in soliciting support for a literary magazine, and with the help of Dr. Bernard "Bunny" Fontana, was able to secure some initial funding through the Doris Duke Oral History Project. Dr. Dozier's daughter, Anya, would later become a student at the University of Arizona and would work with us as a member of the Sun Tracks editorial committee. Following Dr. Dozier, a board of advisors played an important role in helping the students to launch their literary project. The board included, among others, Dr. Fontana, who was with the Arizona State Museum; Dr. Arthur Kay, Virginia Williams, and Dr. Cecil Robinson, all faculty members in the Department of English; and Arline Hobson, a special advisor to American Indian students from the Dean of Students Office.

The following declaration of strength and continuance opened the first issue. It is all we have by way of explaining the name the students chose for their project.

> the Track of the Sun
>   across the Sky
> leaves its shining message,
>   Illuminating,
>   Strengthening,
>   Warming,
> us who are here,
> showing us we are not alone,
>   we are yet ALIVE!
> And this Fire . . .
>   Our fire . . .
> Shall not die!
> *Atoni 1971 (Choctaw)*

Carol Kirk edited the first issue, which was published on August 10, 1971, with help from Armstrong, McKinley, George White (Navajo), and Audrey Peterson (Navajo-Papago). The group believed that the quarterly was "the first American Indian literary publication" (*Tucson Daily Citizen*, Aug. 10, 1971). The founding students announced their purpose as follows: "[*Sun Tracks*] shall be a literary quarterly, which we hope shall prove to be a vehicle for the creative expression of the American Indian people, particularly Indian students. It is our intent that the magazine shall reflect all the American Indian aesthetic heritage, with materials coming from wherever 'The People' may be." To this end, they continued, "we actively solicit contributions from authors and artists, both Indian and non-Indian. The theme of such contributions should relate to some facet of the cultural heritage of the American Indian, either traditional or contemporary."

The momentum of the founding group carried through the publication of two additional issues of volume 1 in the fall of 1971 and the winter of 1971–72. These handsome productions combined strong student writing; the work of Indian writers, such as Gerald Vizenor and N. Scott Momaday, who were then emerging on the national scene; and a selection of photographs and illustrations. During the spring term in 1972, many of the founding students graduated or moved on to other work. A new group of students took up the work for a time. Under the editorship of Faithe C. Seota, they published a fourth and final issue of volume 1 late in 1972.

During the first year I taught at the University of Arizona, 1974–75, I mentioned my admiration for the four issues of *Sun Tracks: An American Indian Literary Quarterly* that had appeared in 1971–1972. Some of the students who had worked on the magazine were still around: could I help them find a way to continue publication? We talked and invited others to join the effort and talked more. Some, like Gerri Keams (Navajo) and Rosita Ruiz (Tohono O'odham), had worked on the first issues. Others had just arrived on campus and were new to the project: Agnes Tso (Navajo), Dan Brudevold (Colville), Dolly Noche (Zuni), Marlene Hoskie (Navajo), and Mike Ladeyo (Hopi). The "we" that became the Sun Tracks editorial committee formed that way.

During this time, 1975 to 1978, Sun Tracks was a project and a place name, as in "Let's go over to Sun Tracks and see what's happening." Where we came together as an editorial committee was around the table: reading manuscripts, joking, arguing over what to accept. There was a lot of laughter, sometimes very intense discussion. People came and went. There seemed to be room at the table for everyone who wanted to be there. We were spared the internecine squabbles that too frequently accompany such projects. Several writers expressed their support early on—Simon Ortiz and Leslie Marmon Silko are two that come immediately to mind. We picked up some help and plenty of advice from people around Tucson. Each issue we published seemed stronger to us than the last. We had the thrill of an expanding audience, accented once in a while by an appreciative note and a subscription from some distant place. The Coordinating Council of Literary Magazines (CCLM) helped us with a couple of small grants. That led to another small grant from the National Endowment for the Arts and an invitation from Ishmael Reed to participate in a distribution project he organized called the Before Columbus Cluster. Our print run of 500 in 1974 grew to 3,000 by 1978.

Students graduated or moved on, and new ones joined the effort. Victor Masayesva, Jr., David Begay, Cathy Gallegos, and especially Marie Levy energized the final year or two that we published as a magazine. With Marie writing letters to stimulate submissions, we heard from more writers, had some more memorable talks around the table—one with Vine Deloria, Jr., we published in volume 4, another with Frank Waters we published in volume 5.

During these years our Sun Tracks office became a supportive home place for Indian students. Dan Brudevold, president of the American Indian Student Club and an active member of the Sun Tracks editorial committee, told a reporter: "It's tough for a lot of the Indian kids to feel a part of the University. When you come from a reservation where you know everyone, this place can be overwhelming. Sun Tracks has made a lot of us feel we made a contribution" (*Arizona Alumnus* 55 [Dec. 1977]: 9).

I remember clearly the events that signaled the end of this phase. We had just published volume 5, an issue graced by Marie's calligraphy and a startling photograph of a Hopi clown boy taken by Owen Seumptewa, and we were feeling pretty good about what we were doing. Then a card came from a metropolitan Indian editor. "Thanks for sending the latest Sun Tracks," the editor wrote. "This one is so beautiful I don't think I'll throw it away. We'll keep it around the office." The perception of what we had been doing as ephemeral was jolting. It seemed that literary magazines were perceived, even by others in the world of little magazines, like newspapers—news today, discarded tomorrow.

About the same time, I recall that there was a lot of discussion, too, about audience: Who were we trying to reach? Were literary magazines the best way to reach readers in the Indian communities all around us? What about doing something that might be more directly aimed at readers in classrooms? How about publishing bilingually in native languages?

We decided to try a book-length project with a focus on four tribes in our area: the Hopi, Navajo, Tohono O'odham, and Yaqui. We recruited editorial committees for each of the four from the students and faculty at the university and urged everybody to go all-out on this one. We made an effort to represent a range of ways that language is used imaginatively in Indian communities. That meant opening up the idea of "Native American literature" to include not just short stories and poems but also songs and stories from the oral tradition, essays, and autobiographical narratives. Ofelia Zepeda led the way in urging that we recognize writing *in* native languages as creative, worthy of publication for its own sake, not just as an instrument for the pursuit of linguistics or anthropology. We made a special effort to find and to publish imaginative writing in each of the four native languages represented in the collection. The result was Sun Tracks Six, *The South Corner of Time*.

The reception of this publication was very positive, both from audiences on the four reservations and from audiences beyond. We had to reprint quickly to meet demand and while the second printing was selling out, we approached the University of Arizona Press with a proposal to reprint *South Corner* as a book. There was reluctance. "We don't publish literature," they said at first. Finally, "because the subject matter has to do with Indians, and anthropology is a strength of our list," they decided *South Corner* was an acceptable addition and the agreement was made. The situation was another stark example of the "Indians are anthropology, not literature" categorization that pervaded university presses and much of the rest of the publishing world into the mid-1980s. Be that as it may, we were happy to be free of the demands of production and distribution and to be able to focus our energies on developing more books.

Reprinting *South Corner* served as the springboard for developing a copublishing relationship with the University of Arizona Press in 1981. We actually inaugurated Sun Tracks as a literary series copublished by the University of Arizona Press in 1982 with the publication of *Mat Hekid O Ju: / When It Rains,* a bilingual book of Tohono O'odham and Pima poetry edited by Ofelia Zepeda, at that time a graduate student in linguistics at the University of Arizona. As an editorial committee to guide the literary series, we drew on the group of Native American graduate students and faculty who came together at the University of Arizona in the early 1980s: Scott Momaday, Vine Deloria, Jr., Leslie Silko, and Emory Sekaquaptewa. Ofelia Zepeda first became involved with Sun Tracks while she was an undergraduate student in a course on American Indian literature I taught. From her work on *South Corner* to the present, she has been an active member of the editorial committee.

The publishing arrangement with the press varied from book to book. We developed different arrangements for different projects. Royalties from *South Corner* and some other projects (notably the *Words and Place* video series) helped us to build a small revolving fund to support the development of Sun Tracks book projects. We used the fund to give authors a small advance or to pay modest contributor's fees, things that the University of Arizona Press was not able to do in those days. We have never had anything like an operating budget from the University of Arizona, although we have been permitted to use office space in several locations along the way. We developed or acquired the manuscripts and took them to the press for editing, design, production, and distribution. We tried to watch over the books as they proceeded through these stages and, depending on the personnel involved, sometimes were able to have considerable input.

The trajectory of our publishing relationship in the early 1990s has clearly been toward increasing assimilation of the Sun Tracks projects into the University of Arizona Press organization. Still, the independent editorial judgments that have been the hallmark of the Sun Tracks projects from the beginning have been maintained in the book series.

In any case, as a book series, Sun Tracks has continued the goals set early on by the literary magazine: to provide publishing opportunities for Native American writers, to be open to publishing the forms of writing and the languages that they choose to work in, to be alert to opportunities to publish both Native American verbal and visual artists, and to strive always for quality. Early on, when *The South Corner of Time* loomed large as a springboard, we tried to develop several book projects that echoed its tribal format. *Spirit Mountain,* a collection from the tribes along the Colorado River (Havasupai, Hualapai, and others) is an example. Like *South Corner,* the general editors, Leanne Hinton and Lucille Watahomigie, utilized different editors for each tribal section. Like *South Corner* and *When It Rains, Spirit Mountain* attempted to recognize and promote writing in native languages. Contacts for the various editorial teams that worked on the book were developed by Ofelia Zepeda, Lucille Watahomigie, and Leanne Hinton during their participation in the American Indian Language Development Institute, a summer institute devoted to the advancement of native literacy. Goals and projects overlapped and became interwoven in this way, but as the Sun Tracks series has progressed there has been nothing like a standard format. We have been opportunistic. Each book has had its own distinctive history. There is not space to tell all those stories here.

Sun Tracks made a transition into another phase in 1992 when

Ofelia Zepeda became Series Editor. Dr. Zepeda, who holds a tenured position in the Linguistics Department at the University of Arizona, continues her long-standing involvement in the American Indian Studies Program, where Sun Tracks is now housed. That Dr. Zepeda will lead Sun Tracks into new areas of emphasis is already clear. On October 15, 1982, in the Tohono O'odham (Papago) Tribal Council Chambers in Sells, Arizona, she arranged an unusual gathering. On that Friday afternoon, many of the tribal offices closed so that workers could attend a special event. The event was certainly the first of its kind: a bilingual poetry reading in O'odham and English to celebrate the publication of *Mat Hekid O Ju: / When It Rains*. As writer after writer came forward to read first in O'odham and then in English, the audience, clearly somewhat wary of this thing called poetry at first, warmed the room with laughter and tears. It was clear that the vision Ofelia and a few others had of creative writing in both Native languages and English was a resounding success. That Ofelia Zepeda has a place in this vital local scene, as well as in the burgeoning national scene in Native American literature, is propitious.

Larry Evers

A SUN TRACKS CHECKLIST

I. *Sun Tracks: An American Indian Literary Quarterly*
Volume 1, number 1 (June 1971), 20 pp.
> Poetry Editor: Carol Kirk; Art and Photography Editor: Orville McKinley; Short Story Editor: David Jackson; Essay Editor: Mini Kaczkurkin; Secretary: Teresa Wall; Business Manager: George White; Special Projects: Roy Armstrong and Rachel Bonney; Public Relations: Audrey Peterson, Anthony DeClay, and Lawrence Isaac.

Contributors: Atoni, Liz Sohappy, O. McKinley, Patty Leah Harjo, William A. Roecker, Grey Cohoe, Gerald Robert Vizenor, Stephan Wall, Sam Tayah, Laura Chee, Jon Colvin, Louise Brown, Robert Chee.

Volume 1, number 2 (Fall 1971), 32 pp.

Managing Editor: Roy Armstrong; Literary Editor: George White; Art: Orville McKinley and Mike Wise; Business Affairs: Audrey Peterson and Rachel Bonney; Staff: Faithe Seota, Teresa Wall, Thomasine Hill, Martin McGaughey, Mini Kaczkurkin, and Rosita Ruiz.

Contributors: Patricia Irving, Virgil Curtis Link, Johnny Romero, Ravensblood, Patty Leah Harjo, Gerald Vizenor, Atoni, Ruth W. Giddings, Helen Sekaquaptewa, Louise Udall, Faithe Seota, Helga Teiwes, M. Wise, O. McKinley, Trudy Griffin, Robert Chee, R. Armstrong.

Volume 1, number 3 (Winter 1971–72), 32 pp.

Managing Editor: Roy A. Armstrong; Literary Editor: George White; Assistant Editor: Faithe Seota; Art: Trudy Griffin, Thomas Yazzie, and Peter Deswood; Business: Audrey Peterson; Subscriptions: Rachel Bonney; Staff: Thomasine Hill, Geraldine Keams, Rosita Ruiz, Orville McKinley, Teresa Wall, Larry Isaac, and Phyllis Chatham.

Contributors: Scott Momaday, M. Leon-Portilla, Alberta Nofchissey, Phil George, King Kuka, Harry Levantonio, R. J. Johnson, Rudy Bantista, Bruce Ignacio, Johnny Harvey, Patty Harjo, Shirley Woody, Sharon Burnette, Francis Brazil, Greta Sullateskee, Sherry Hampton, Ted Palmanteer, Larry Bird, Alonzo Lopez, T. Yazzi, P. Deswood, S. Peters, O. McKinley, T. Griffin, and Atoni.

Volume 1, number 4 (Spring 1972), 32 pp.

(This number was misprinted as "volume 1, number 3")

Managing Editor: Faithe C. Seota; Assistant Editor: Larry
Curley; Art: Trudy Griffin, Orville McKinley, and Larry
Isaac; Subscriptions: Rachel Bonney; Staff: Geraldine Keams
and Rosita Ruiz.

Contributors: Red Bird, Gerri Keams, Patty Harjo, Liz Sohappy,
Larry Emerson, Vance Goodiron, No-Nee, Agustin Nasewy-
tewa, Johnny Charlie, Richard Thaylor, Donnie Yellowfly,
Roger Lee, Tony Tsosie, Trudy Griffin, and Robert Bautista.

II. *Sun Tracks: An American Indian Literary Magazine*
Volume 2, number 1 (Fall 1975), 25 pp.

Editorial Committee: Daniel Brudevold, Dr. Larry Evers, James
Hepworth, Eva Kahn, Michael Ladeyo, Dolly Noche, Rosita
Ruiz, and Agnes Tso.

Contributors: Agnes Tso, Simon J. Ortiz, Yilhazba, Gerri
Keams, Angelita Kisto Maldonado, Darrell Rumbley, Nia
Francisco, Alicia Kavena, Michael Ladeyo, and Joyotpaul
Chaudhuri.

Volume 2, number 2 (Spring 1976), 25 pp.

Editorial Committee: Dan Brudevold, Eva K. Castillo, Larry
Evers, James Hepworth, Marlene Hoskie, Dolly Noche,
Wayne Taylor, Jr., and Agnes Tso.

Contributors: Refugio Savala, Charles R. Ballard, Paula Gunn
Allen, Simon J. Ortiz, Ray Young Bear, Mini Valenzuela
Kaczkurkin, Carter Revard, and N. Scott Momaday.

Volume 3, number 1 (Fall 1976), 37 pp.

Editorial Committee: Dan Brudevold, Lena Begay, Larry Evers,
James Hepworth, Marlene Hoskie, Emma Jim, Wilhelmina
Jim, Dolly Noche, Wayne Taylor, Jr., and Agnes Tso.

Contributors: A. Kelsey, N. Scott Momaday, Hiram R. Smith, Aaron Yava, William Oandasan, Gerald Hobson, Yolanda Schultz, nila northsun, Robert Conley, Roman Adrian, Leslie Marmon Silko, and Duane BigEagle.

Volume 3, number 2 (Spring 1977), 40 pp.

Editorial Committee: Elena Bennett, Dan Brudevold, Steve Crum, Larry Evers, Jim Hepworth, Marlene Hoskie, Emma Jim, Calvin Kelly, Alex Mendez, Dolly Noche, Myrna Pavatea, Barbara Sorrell, and Wayne Taylor.

Contributors: Norman BigEagle, Duane BigEagle, Alexander Posey, Joe Sando, George Hood, Louise Abeita, Rick Casillas, Simon J. Ortiz, Lance Henson, Nora Naranjo, Juan Reyna, Liz Cook, and Barney Bush, with a Special Section of Writing by Indian Young People.

Volume 4, *Sun Tracks Four: Native American Perspectives* (1978)

Edited by Larry Evers, Marlene Hoskie, Roberta Howard, and Victor Masayesva.

Contributors: Leslie Silko, Victor Masayesva, Luci Tapahonso, Roberta Hill, Tim Clashin, Albert Yuhmayo, Arlene McGee, Jon West, Fillman Childs Bell, Jim Sagel, Maurice Kenny, Barney Bush, and Vine Deloria, Jr.

Volume 5, *Suntracks Five* (1979)

Edited by Larry Evers, Marie Levy, David Begay, and Kathy Gallegos.

Contributors: Emory Sekaquaptewa, Owen Seumptewa, Harold Littlebird, nila northsun, Jim Sagel, Blair Hess, Craig Volk, Michael Dorris, Jim Barnes, Cynthia Wilson, Linda Hogan, Lomawywesa (Michael Kabotie), Geri Felix, Frank Waters, and Kenji Kawano.

Volume 6, *The South Corner of Time: Hopi, Navajo, Papago, and Yaqui Tribal Literature* (1980), 240 pp.

> Edited by Larry Evers, with Anaya Dozier, Danny Lopez, Felipe Molina, Ellavina Tsosie Perkins, Emory Sekaquaptewa, and Ofelia Zepeda.
>
> Contributors: Albert Yava, Emory Sekaquaptewa, Owen Seumptewa, Herschel Talashoma, Edmund Nequatewa, Ekkehart Malotki, Wendy Rose, Lomawywesa, Victor Masa-yesva, Irene Nakai, Sandoval, Tom Ration, Kenji Kawano, Nancy Woodman, Betty John, Agnes Tso, Nia Francisco, Gary Witherspoon, Andrew Natonabah, Martha Austin, Ventura José, Danny Lopez, Alice Listo, Frank Lopez, Ted Rios, Kathleen Sands, Tony Celentano, Ruth Underhill, Susie Ignacio Enos, Ofelia Zepeda, Geri Felix, Anselmo Valencia, Felipe Molina, Carmen Garcia, Ruth Giddings, Paula Castillo, Mini Valenzuela Kaczkurkin, and Refugio Savala.

Mini Valenzuela Kaczkurkin. *Yoeme: Lore of the Arizona Yaqui People*. A Sun Tracks Book. Tucson, Ariz.: Sun Tracks, 1977.

> This book evolved from a project Mini Valenzuela did for a folklore class I taught in the 1970s. Mini wanted to get it printed for use in her work as a storyteller in the local school districts. Some other members of the Sun Tracks editorial committee and I assisted Mini by helping her with the editing and by advancing some money for the design and typesetting and a first run. The book quickly paid for itself. Then, happily, Mini Valenzuela took over, had the book reprinted at least two more times, and sold the copies herself.

III. *Sun Tracks: An American Indian Literary Series*
Published by Sun Tracks and the University of Arizona Press
Series Editor: Larry Evers (1981–1991)

Editorial Advisory Committee: Vine Deloria, Jr., Joy Harjo, N. Scott Momaday, Emory Sekaquaptewa, Leslie Marmon Silko, and Ofelia Zepeda.

Volume 6: Larry Evers, ed. *The South Corner of Time: Hopi, Navajo, Papago, and Yaqui Tribal Literature.* 1981. Reprint of *Sun Tracks,* volume 6.

Volume 7: Ofelia Zepeda, ed. *Mat Hekid O Ju: 'O'odham Ha-Cegitodag / When It Rains: Papago and Pima Poetry.* 1982.

Volume 8: Victor Masayesva, Jr., and Erin Younger, eds. *Hopi Photographers / Hopi Images.* 1983.

Volume 9: Herschel Talashoma, narrator. *Hopitutuwutsi: Hopi Tales.* Translated by Ekkehart Malotki. 1983.

Volume 10: Leanne Hinton and Lucille J. Watahomigie, eds. *Spirit Mountain: An Anthology of Yuman Story and Song.* 1984.

Volume 11: Sam and Janet Bingham, eds. *Between Sacred Mountains: Navajo Stories and Lessons from the Land.* 1984.

Volume 12: Simon J. Ortiz. *A Good Journey.* 1984.

Volume 13: James McCarthy. *A Papago Traveler: The Memories of James McCarthy.* Edited by John G. Westover. 1985.

Volume 14: Larry Evers and Felipe S. Molina. *Yaqui Deer Songs / Maso Bwikam: A Native American Poetry.* 1987.

Volume 15: Joseph Bruchac. *Survival This Way: Interviews with American Indian Poets.* 1987.

Volume 16: N. Scott Momaday. *The Names: A Memoir.* 1987.

Volume 17: Joy Harjo and Stephen Strom. *Secrets from the Center of the World.* 1989.

Volume 18: Bernd C. Peyer, ed. *The Singing Spirit: Early Short Stories by North American Indians.* 1989.

Volume 19: Andrea Lerner, ed. *Dancing on the Rim of the World: An Anthology of Contemporary Northwest Native American Writing.* 1990.

IV. *Sun Tracks: An American Indian Literary Series*
Published by the University of Arizona Press
Series Editors: Ofelia Zepeda and Larry Evers (1991–93)
Editorial Advisory Committee: Vine Deloria, Jr., Joy Harjo, N. Scott Momaday, Emory Sekaquaptewa, and Leslie Marmon Silko
Volume 20: Nora Naranjo-Morse. *Mud Woman: Poems from the Clay.* 1992.

Volume 21: Simon J. Ortiz. *Woven Stone.* 1992.

Volume 22: D'Arcy McNickle. *The Hawk Is Hungry and Other Stories.* Edited by Birgit Hans. 1992.

Volume 23: Luci Tapahonso. *Sáanii Dahataał / The Women Are Singing: Poems and Stories.* 1993.

Series Editor: Ofelia Zepeda (1993 to the present)
Editorial Advisory Committee: Vine Deloria, Jr., Larry Evers, Joy Harjo, N. Scott Momaday, Emory Sekaquaptewa, and Leslie Marmon Silko
Volume 24: Carter Revard. *An Eagle Nation.* 1993.

Volume 25: Ruth Underhill. *Singing for Power: The Song Magic of the Papago Indians of Southern Arizona.* 1993.

Volume 26: Greg Sarris, ed. *The Sound of Rattles and Clappers: A Collection of New California Indian Painting.* 1994.

Volume 27: Wendy Rose. *Bone Dance: New and Selected Poems, 1965–1993.* 1994.

Volume 28: Simon J. Ortiz. *After and Before the Lightning.* 1994.

Volume 29: Joseph Bruchac, ed. *Returning the Gift: Poetry and Prose from the First North American Native Writers' Festival.* 1994.

Volume 30: Elizabeth Woody. *Luminaries of the Humble.* 1994.

Volume 31: Larry Evers and Ofelia Zepeda, eds. *Home Places: Contemporary Native American Writing from Sun Tracks.* 1995.

Volume 32: Ofelia Zepeda. *Ocean Power: Poems from the Desert.* 1995.

Contributors

George Blueeyes, also known as Tabaahi Ts'osi, is a medicine man living at Rock Point, Arizona. He was born about 1900 and is Tabaahi Clan (his mother's clan), born for Tl'izi Lani (his father's clan). His grandmother, Red Woman, was also Tl'izi Lani—the Many Goats Clan—and was a close relative of Old Man Hat. A respected elder, he worked closely with Sam and Janet Bingham, Rex Lee Jim, and the others who wrote *Between Sacred Mountains* for the Rock Point Community School.

Ralph Cameron was born in Laveen, Arizona. At the age of six he was sent to a boarding school in California for a year, but he returned to Arizona to finish his schooling at the Phoenix Indian School. He spent most of his adult life in Los Angeles working in a steel factory. When he retired, he returned to Laveen, where he became an active member of his community. With many other elders, he has been actively working to record as much as possible of the Maricopa language and culture and to begin a language program for the children.

Larry Evers, a professor in the Department of English at the University of Arizona, produced *Words and Place* (1979), a series of videotapes of American Indian singers, storytellers, and authors. With Felipe S. Molina, he has published such works as *Yaqui Deer Songs / Maso Bwikam* (Sun Tracks series, 1987), *Woi' Bwikam / Coyote Songs* (1990), and "Hiakim: The Yaqui Homeland" (*Journal of the Southwest* 34 [1992]: 1–138).

Dan Hanna learned many songs and stories from his father, Henry Hanna, and even more from his uncle, Mark Hanna, a shaman. Until his untimely death in 1968, Dan Hanna was respected as one of the best and most knowledgeable singers among the Havasupai, specializing in traditional tales, sweathouse songs, and medicine songs. Dan Hanna left the canyon where the Havasupai live for ten years under a government project to relocate people in cities. He lived and worked in Los Angeles during that time, but then he came back to his canyon home, where he stayed until he died. He is survived by many children and grandchildren.

Joy Harjo is a professor in the Creative Writing Program at the University of New Mexico. Her books include *In Mad Love and War* (1990), *She Had Some Horses* (1983), and *What Moon Drove Me to This?* (1979). Joy Harjo is also a musician and the leader of the band Poetic Justice.

Lance Henson, a member of the Cheyenne Dog Soldier Society and a veteran of Vietnam, lives near Calumet, Oklahoma. His *Selected Poems, 1970–1983* was published in 1985. "The Whirlwind Is a Mirror: An Interview with Lance Henson" appears in Joseph Bruchac's *Survival This Way: Interviews with American Indian Poets* (Sun Tracks series, 1987).

Linda Hogan is a professor in the Creative Writing Program at the University of Colorado, Boulder. Her novel *Mean Spirit* was published in 1990. Her books of poetry include *Calling Myself Home* (1978), *Eclipse* (1983), and *Seeing through the Sun* (1985). Extended interviews with Linda Hogan appear in Laura Coltelli's *Winged Words: American Indian Writers Speak* (1990) and Joseph Bruchac's *Survival This Way* (1987).

Daniel Lopez lives in Big Fields, Arizona, and works as a teacher in Sells on the Tohono O'odham reservation where he was born and raised. An active singer, he has been instrumental in educating many young people in Tohono O'odam language and literature.

Felipe S. Molina grew up in the Yaqui settlement near Marana, Arizona, which is now called Yoem Pueblo. He credits his grandmother, Anselma Angwis Tonopuamea, and his grandfather, Rosario Bacaneri Castillo, who was a famous pahkola (a ritual clown and orator), with educating him in the Yaqui language and ways. An active deer singer, he has served as governor of Yoem Pueblo, as a member of the Pascua Yaqui Tribal Council, and on numerous projects designed to promote Yaqui language and culture. He has written numerous articles and books, including *Yaqui Deer Songs / Maso Bwikam* (Sun Tracks series, 1987), *Woi Bwikam / Coyote Songs* (1990), and *Hiakim: The Yaqui Homeland* (1992), all of which were co-authored with Larry Evers.

N. Scott Momaday, Regents Professor of English at the University of Arizona, has published numerous books and articles. They include *In the Presence of the Sun* (1992), *The Ancient Child* (1989), *The Way to Rainy Mountain* (1969), and *House Made of Dawn* (1968), which won the Pulitzer Prize in 1969. "The Indolent Boys," a play, was produced at Harvard University in 1992. N. Scott Momaday is also an active painter whose work has been exhibited internationally.

Nora Naranjo-Morse is a sculptor and a poet. Her sculpture has been widely exhibited nationally and internationally. *Mud Woman: Poems from the Clay* was published by the University of Arizona in the Sun Tracks series in 1992. Nora Naranjo-Morse's work is discussed in Stephen Trimble's *Talking with the Clay: The Art of Pueblo Pottery* (1987) and Linda B. Eaton's *A Separate Vision: Case Studies of Four Contemporary Indian Artists* (1990).

Simon J. Ortiz was born and raised on Acoma Pueblo lands in New Mexico. A prolific writer, he has published many books, among them *From Sand Creek* (1981), *Fightin'* (1983), *The People Shall Continue* (1988), and *Woven Stone* (University of Arizona Press, 1992). Laura

Coltelli published an extended interview with him in *Winged Words: American Indian Writers Speak* (1990). *Before and After the Lightning* (1994), his most recent work, is set on the Rosebud Reservation in South Dakota and was published by the University of Arizona Press in the Sun Tracks series in 1994.

Carter Revard grew up in Buck Creek on the Osage Reservation in Oklahoma, and he is now a professor of English at Washington University in St. Louis. Two collections of his poetry have been published: *Ponca War Dancers* (1980) and *Cowboys and Indians, Christmas Shopping* (1992). His poetry collection *An Eagle Nation* was published in the Sun Tracks series in 1993. Revard's numerous essays include "Traditional Osage Naming Ceremonies: Entering the Circle of Being," in *Recovering the Word* (1987) and an autobiographical portrait in *I Tell You Now: Autobiographical Essays by Native American Writers* (1987).

Wendy Rose was born in Oakland, California, in 1948. Her tribal affiliations are Hopi and Miwok. She has been the coordinator and an instructor of American Indian Studies at Fresno City College since 1984. She is the author of twelve books of poetry. Her book *Bone Dance: New and Selected Poems, 1965–1993*, was published by the University of Arizona Press in the Sun Tracks series in 1994.

Refugio Savala was a poet, writer, and translator. He was the author of *The Autobiography of a Yaqui Poet*, which was edited by Kathleen M. Sands (University of Arizona Press, 1980). His book offers a unique view of the Arizona Yaqui, as well as a narrative of the personal and artistic growth of a Native American man of letters. Savala died in 1991.

Luci Tapahonso was born and raised in Shiprock, New Mexico, and is member of the Navajo Nation. She has taught at the University of

New Mexico and Navajo Community College and is presently an associate professor of English at the University of Kansas. She has published four books of poetry: *One More Shiprock Night* (1981), *Seasonal Woman* (1982), *A Breeze Swept Through* (1987), and *Sáanii Dahataał / The Women Are Singing: Poems and Stories* (Sun Tracks series, 1993). In 1987 her autobiographical essay "A Sense of Myself" was published in *Dine Be'iina'*, a Navajo studies journal published by the Navajo Community College, in Shiprock. Joseph Bruchac published "For What It Is: An Interview with Luci Tapahonso" in *Survival This Way* (Sun Tracks series, 1987).

Georgiana Valoyce-Sanchez is Chumash and O'odham and is a recognized member of the Coastal Band of the Chumash Nation. She was born and raised in California and currently teaches American Indian literature at California State University at Long Beach. Her poetry manuscript, *A Light To Do Shellwork By*, is dedicated to her father, a respected Chumash elder who died on August 15, 1991.

Ramona Wilson, a member of the Colville Confederated Tribes, was born in Nespelem, Washington. She is now a teacher and project director for the American Indian Bilingual Program in the Oakland, California, public schools.

Elizabeth Woody, a Warm Springs, Wasco/Navajo Indian, majored in creative writing at the Institute of American Indian Arts in Santa Fe. *Hand Into Stone*, her first volume of poetry, was published in 1988. She is a founding member of the Northwest Native Writers' Association. Her autobiographical narrative "By Our Hand, Through the Memory, the House Is More Than Form" appeared in *A Circle of Nations: Voices and Visions of American Indians* (1993). Her collection of poems *Luminaries of the Humble* was published as part of the Sun Tracks series in 1994.

Ofelia Zepeda was born near the Tohono O'odham reservation in Stanfield, Arizona. A professor in the Linguistics Department and the American Indian Studies Program at the University of Arizona, she has published a number of studies of the O'odham language and directs the American Indian Language Development Institute, an annual summer institute for American Indian teachers. Her book of poetry, *Ocean Power*, is a volume in the Sun Tracks series. She is series editor of Sun Tracks.

Acknowledgments

George Blueeyes' "Sacred Mountains" was published in *Between Sacred Mountains: Navajo Stories and Lessons from the Land*, edited by Sam Bingham and Janet Bingham, Sun Tracks, vol. 11 (1984).

Ralph Cameron's "My Land" was published in *Spirit Mountain: An Anthology of Yuman Story and Song*, edited by Leanne Hinton and Lucille Watahomigie, Sun Tracks, vol. 10 (1984).

Dan Hanna's "Medicine Song" was published in *Spirit Mountain: An Anthology of Yuman Story and Song*, edited by Leanne Hinton and Lucille J. Watahomigie, Sun Tracks, vol. 10 (1984).

Joy Harjo's "My House Is the Red Earth" was published in *Secrets from the Center of the World*, by Joy Harjo, with photographs by Stephen Strom, Sun Tracks, vol. 17 (1989).

Lance Henson's "Glimpse of Home" was published in *Sun Tracks*, vol. 3, no. 2 (Spring 1977).

Linda Hogan's "Water Rising" was published in *Sun Tracks*, vol. 5 (1979).

Daniel Lopez's "Lonely Mountain" was published in *Mat Hekid O Ju: 'O'odham Ha-Cegitodag/When It Rains: Papago and Pima Poetry*, edited by Ofelia Zepeda, Sun Tracks, vol. 7 (1982).

Felipe S. Molina's "Flower-Covered Fawn" was published in *Yaqui Deer Songs / Maso Bwikam: A Native American Poetry*, by Larry Evers and Felipe S. Molina, Sun Tracks, vol. 14 (1987).

N. Scott Momaday's "From My Home of Jemez" was published in *The Names: A Memoir* (New York: Harper & Row, 1976; reprint, Sun Tracks, vol. 16 [1987]).

Nora Naranjo-Morse's "Ta" was published in *Mud Woman: Poems from the Clay*, Sun Tracks, vol. 20 (1992).

Simon J. Ortiz's "That's the Place Indians Talk About" was published in *Fight Back: For the Sake of the People, For the Sake of the Land*, vol. 1, no. 1, of the *INAD Literary Journal* (Institute for Native American Development, Native American Studies, University of New Mexico, 1980), and reprinted in *Woven Stone*, Sun Tracks, vol. 21 (1992).

Carter Revard's "An Eagle Nation" was published in *An Eagle Nation*, Sun Tracks, vol. 24 (1993).

Wendy Rose's "The Endangered Roots of a Person" was published in *The Sound of Rattles and Clappers: A Collection of New California Indian Writing*, edited by Greg Sarris, Sun Tracks, vol. 26 (1994).

Refugio Savala's "Growth: Merging of Labor and Love" was published in *The Autobiography of a Yaqui Poet* (University of Arizona Press, 1980) and reprinted in *The South Corner of Time: Hopi, Navajo, Papago, Yaqui Tribal Literature*, edited by Larry Evers, Sun Tracks, vol. 6 (1981).

Luci Tapahonso's "The Motion of Songs Rising" was published in *Sáanii Dahataał/The Women Are Singing: Poems and Stories*, Sun Tracks, vol. 23 (1993).

Georgiana Valoyce-Sanchez's "Fat of the Land" was published in *The Sound of Rattles and Clappers: A Collection of New California Indian Writing*, edited by Greg Sarris, Sun Tracks, vol. 26 (1994).

Ramona Wilson's "December on the Coast" was published in *Dancing on the Rim of the World: An Anthology of Contemporary Northwest Native American Writing*, edited by Andrea Lerner, Sun Tracks, vol. 19 (1990).

Elizabeth Woody's "In the Memory of Crossing the Columbia" was published in *Dancing on the Rim of the World: An Anthology of Contemporary Northwest Native American Writing*, edited by Andrea Lerner, Sun Tracks, vol. 19 (1990).

Ofelia Zepeda's "Pulling Down the Clouds" was published in *Returning the Gift: Poetry and Prose from the First North American Native Writers' Festival*, edited by Joseph Bruchac, Sun Tracks, vol. 29 (1994).